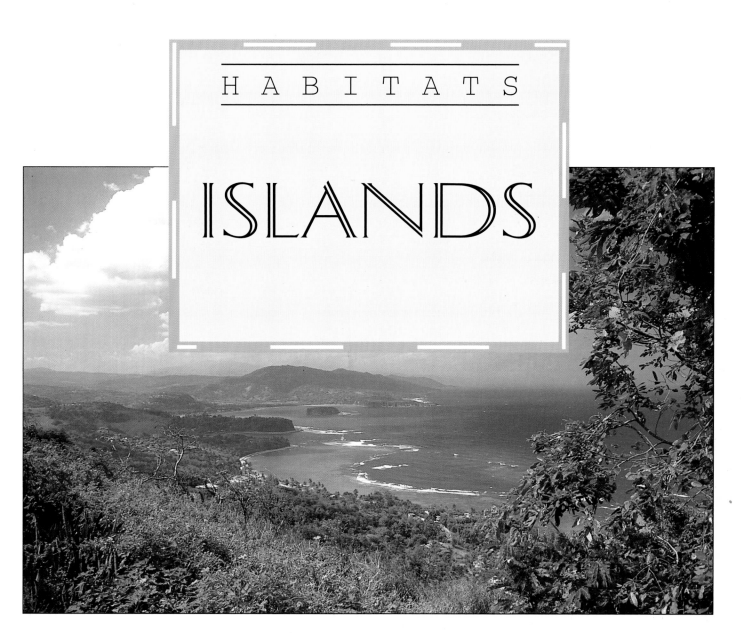

HABITATS

ISLANDS

JULIA WATERLOW

Thomson Learning
New York

HABITATS

Deserts
Islands
Mountains
Polar Regions
Rivers and Lakes
Wetlands

Cover: An aerial view of islands in a warm tropical sea
Contents page: The Komodo Dragon of Indonesia

First published in the United States in 1995 by
Thomson Learning
New York, NY

Published simultaneously in Great Britain by Wayland (Publishers) Ltd.

U.S. copyright © 1995 Thomson Learning

U.K. copyright © 1995 Wayland (Publishers) Ltd.

Library of Congress Cataloging-in-Publication Data
Waterlow, Julia.
Islands / Julia Waterlow.
        p.   cm.—(Habitats)
   Includes bibliographical references and index.
   ISBN 1-56847-387-7
   1. Islands—Juvenile literature. [1. Islands. 2. Island ecology.
3. Ecology.] I. Title. II. Series.
GB471.W38   1995
333.73—dc20   95-4027

Printed in Italy

CONTENTS

1. SURROUNDED BY WATER

Far from land, hidden among the vast watery expanses of the oceans, islands conjure up dreams of mystery, adventure, and beauty. For some people they are a kind of paradise, covered with palm trees, fringed by sandy beaches, and surrounded by clear, warm blue seas. In fact there are still thousands of small islands in far-off places, uninhabited and little visited by people, that fit this romantic ideal. However, in the modern world many islands have become important and busy centers of trade, heavily built-up and densely populated.

The general name given to the place where plants or animals live is called their habitat. An island differs from other habitats because it is surrounded on all sides by water. If the island is a long way from the mainland, the water can act like a barrier. As a result, some islands support their own special animals and plants that may not be found anywhere else. The fact that islands may be isolated from the rest of the world can affect the way the human island population has developed, too.

This map indicates some of the world's larger islands and island groups.

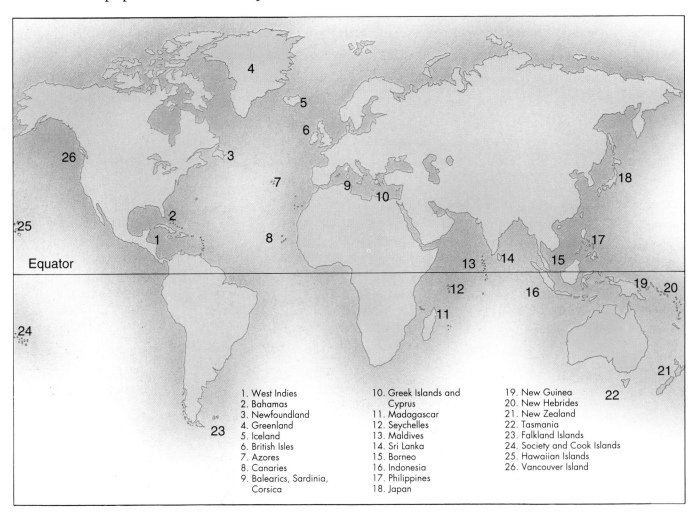

1. West Indies
2. Bahamas
3. Newfoundland
4. Greenland
5. Iceland
6. British Isles
7. Azores
8. Canaries
9. Balearics, Sardinia, Corsica
10. Greek Islands and Cyprus
11. Madagascar
12. Seychelles
13. Maldives
14. Sri Lanka
15. Borneo
16. Indonesia
17. Philippines
18. Japan
19. New Guinea
20. New Hebrides
21. New Zealand
22. Tasmania
23. Falkland Islands
24. Society and Cook Islands
25. Hawaiian Islands
26. Vancouver Island

Left Sun, sand, and palm trees, surrounded by clear water—this is perhaps the ideal tropical island.

Although islands have in common the fact that they are each surrounded by water, the habitats they provide are varied. There is every type of landscape, from ice-covered lumps of rock near the North and South Poles to the lush tropical forests of islands close to the equator. In many cases, it is not just the climate but the way the island was formed that allows certain types of plants and animals to survive.

Besides their physical characteristics, islands have also been shaped by history, politics, and economics. Outsiders have appeared, conquering, invading, or trading and have changed the way of life for native islanders forever. On many islands new plants and animals have been introduced, permanently altering the islands' native species. As in many parts of the world, the natural resources of islands are being heavily exploited. Care of the environment is of special concern because most islands have fragile ecologies and the natural balance can be easily upset.

Below The heart of New York City is crammed onto Manhattan Island.

2. ISLAND FORMS

Although all islands are surrounded by water, it is not always the sea; islands are also found in lakes and rivers. Some islands have existed for millions of years. Others only appear for a short space of time, perhaps a few hundred years or even less, and are quickly eroded away by the forces of nature, disappearing under the sea if the water level rises or if the earth's crust sinks.

There are four main ways that islands can form. Land sometimes becomes separated from the mainland, or a mound of earth is built up as mud or sand is deposited by water. Other islands are formed by volcanic action or by the growth of coral.

Continental islands

Many islands, often those lying near a continent, were once joined to the mainland. About 220 million years ago, the continents as we know them today were part of a huge landmass called Pangaea. This landmass gradually broke up, and the pieces, or continents, drifted apart, eventually reaching their present positions and shapes. As this happened, smaller pieces separated from the larger continents and became islands surrounded by sea. The huge island of Madagascar, off the southeast coast of Africa, was formed in this way. About 160 million years ago, the island broke away from the African continent and has been separated ever since by a 250-mile strait of water.

Sea level changes have also left pieces of land that were once part of a continent separated by water. One reason the sea level varies in height is that the climate of the earth is constantly changing. The last cold period,

A diagram showing the break-up of continents

200 million years ago. At this time, there was only one huge landmass surrounded by ocean. India was wedged between Africa and Australia.

65 million years ago. As the huge landmass gradually broke up, pieces of it drifted apart. Oceans were formed, separating the continents. Very gradually, over millions of years, the continents moved position.

Today. The continents are in their present familiar position. India has drifted to join Europe and Asia, and Australia has drifted far away from the original landmass.

the last Ice Age, peaked about 18,000 years ago. Freezing temperatures turned the seas to ice, and massive sheets of ice several miles thick moved out from the poles. So much water was locked up as ice that it is thought the level of the sea was more than 400 feet lower than it is now. When the earth warmed again, the ice melted and raised the level of water in the sea all over the world.

Great Britain and most of its many islands were once linked by a land bridge with the European continent. During the last 8,000 years, after the end of the last Ice Age, the sea level gradually rose, flooding valleys and lowland areas until the British Isles became completely separated from Europe by the English Channel. Sri Lanka, Tasmania, Taiwan, and many of North America's east coast islands, such as Manhattan and Newfoundland, were also once part of the mainland they adjoin.

Sedimentary islands

Islands can appear where mud or soil is deposited in great quantities. Off the coasts of the Netherlands, Germany, and Denmark lie the Frisian Islands, a chain of low sandy islands. Sand and soil were gradually dumped along this part of the coast by the sea, forming sand dunes. These were slowly broken up and separated from the mainland by storms. Today there is a shallow sea between the islands and the mainland. They support good grazing for cattle but are too sandy and windswept for trees to grow.

Islands often appear near the mouths of rivers. These are usually made up of sediment, the mud and earth carried by a river. In its early stages, a river is fast flowing and powerful and erodes the surrounding earth and rock, carrying pieces away downstream with the water. A river slows near the end of its course, and, as it does so, it begins to drop its load of sediment on the riverbed. In some places so much sediment is deposited that it forms a mound of mud and soil that grows into an island.

In Brazil, in the mouth of the Amazon River lies Marajó Island, the largest river delta island in the world. It is nearly the size of Switzerland. Large parts of the island are regularly flooded in the wet season, although enough remains permanently dry for people to live on the island and for trees to grow.

One of the Frisian Islands off the coast of Germany. These islands were formed by soil and sand deposited over thousands of years.

Volcanic islands

Thousands of the world's islands were and still are being created by volcanic activity. Nearly all islands lying in the middle of oceans appeared in this way.

Underneath the crust of our planet it is so hot that the rocks and minerals are molten liquid. On top of this is the earth's surface, which is made up of a series of solid plates that float and slowly move around. Where the plates meet and rub together are areas where the crust is weakest and the molten interior of the earth can spill out, sometimes in a volcanic explosion or at other times in a seeping flow of lava. Many of the earth's plates meet under the sea. Often the volcanic activity at these points throws up ash and lava that solidifies when it cools on contact with the air or water. Where the eruption is big enough, an island emerges out of the sea.

Most of the world's volcanic islands appear in the Pacific Ocean, where the vast Pacific plate collides with other larger and smaller plates. One of the

An appearing and disappearing island
In the eighteenth century, Falcon Island, near Tonga, in the Pacific Ocean, was recorded as a reef. In 1885 the island rose 240 feet above sea level, but by 1899 it had disappeared again because of erosion. In 1927 a volcanic eruption raised the island again to a height of 300 feet above sea level, but by 1949 it had sunk once more.

Gray lava fills a crater on Kilauea volcano, Hawaii, an island in the middle of the Pacific Ocean.

best-known Pacific islands is Hawaii. It is one of a line of volcanic islands, the first of which, Kauai, appeared about five-and-one-half million years ago. Hawaii is the youngest in the chain, appearing about one million years ago. It has three volcanoes, the highest rising to more than 13,000 feet above sea level. Kilauea volcano still oozes molten lava; the last major flow occurred in 1990.

Volcanic islands can appear and disappear overnight or take hundreds of years to appear as the lava slowly builds up. One of the newest and quickest island arrivals was the island of Surtsey, in the North Atlantic not far from Iceland. Surtsey lies along another important oceanic line of volcanic activity, the Mid-Atlantic Ridge. In November 1963 lava started bulging up out of the sea. Suddenly, a five-mile-high column of steam, ash, and fumes poured out; at some moments, rocks were being thrown out from the volcano at a rate of half a million tons per hour. In two days the island was 125 feet high; within a week it had reached more than 325 feet high and about a half a mile long. The eruptions finally stopped in 1967, leaving an island almost two miles in length.

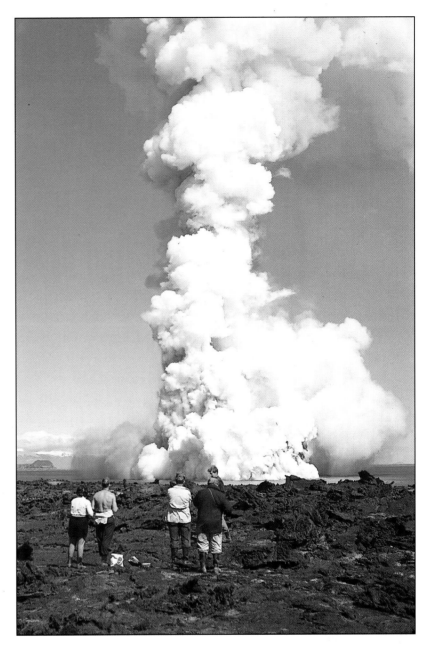

Spectators on Surtsey watch a nearby volcanic island erupting out of the sea.

Island explosion
On August 28, 1883, hot molten rock and ash were blasted into the stratosphere, some of it 50 miles high. In a few seconds the volcanic island of Krakatoa disappeared as it collapsed, causing the biggest natural explosion ever recorded. The deafening noise even reached Australia, more than 3,000 miles away. The explosion caused a huge tidal wave and a wall of water the height of a four-story house, traveling at 300 mph. It wrecked the shores of the island of Java nearby; in South Africa, 5,000 miles away, boats were rocked at anchor.

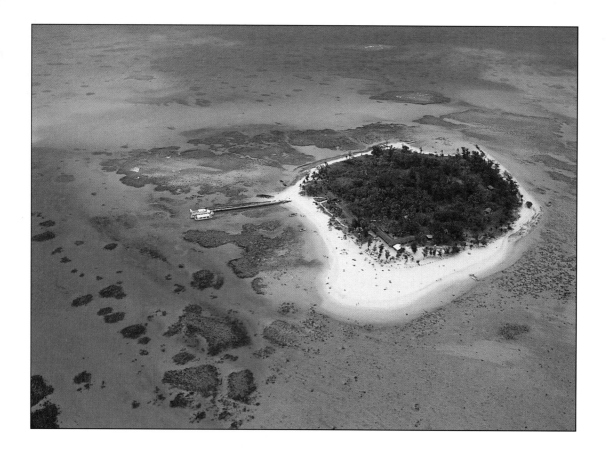

A coral island surrounded by reefs, in the Mariana Islands in the Pacific Ocean.

Coral islands

There is one type of island that is actually made by living creatures: the coral island. Millions of tiny animals build tough shell-like homes, one on top of another, to form a reef, a kind of hard underwater bank, in the sea. Should the seabed rise or sea level fall even slightly, these reefs are left above the sea as islands.

Coral likes shallow, clear, and warm water and is often found growing around volcanic islands in tropical seas. Many islands of the Pacific and

A diagram showing the formation of a coral atoll.

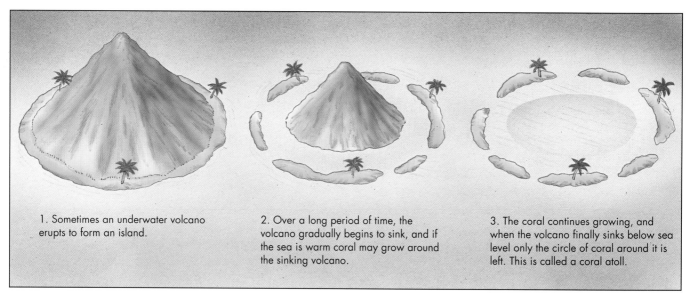

1. Sometimes an underwater volcano erupts to form an island.

2. Over a long period of time, the volcano gradually begins to sink, and if the sea is warm coral may grow around the sinking volcano.

3. The coral continues growing, and when the volcano finally sinks below sea level only the circle of coral around it is left. This is called a coral atoll.

Indian oceans are made of coral. Coral grows incredibly slowly—even in the warmest waters it only grows six to ten feet in a century. It can happen that a volcanic island slowly drops back into the ocean and only the coral ring that has grown around the volcano is left, making a circle of coral reefs. This is called an atoll, and can be anything from a few miles across to more than a hundred miles across. The reef is seldom continuous. It usually has breaks in it, channels that allow boats to sail through into the inner lagoon.

Aldabra is an atoll in the Seychelles, lying 250 miles east of Africa. It is less than 20 miles long and easy to miss in the seas of the great Indian Ocean. Its huge lagoon is encircled by a ring of coral islets that sit like a cap on an underwater volcano rising 13,000 feet from the seabed below. Aldabra is known to have appeared above the water and dropped below its surface several times as the sea level or ocean floor has risen or fallen; its rise to its present height is thought to have begun about 50,000 years ago.

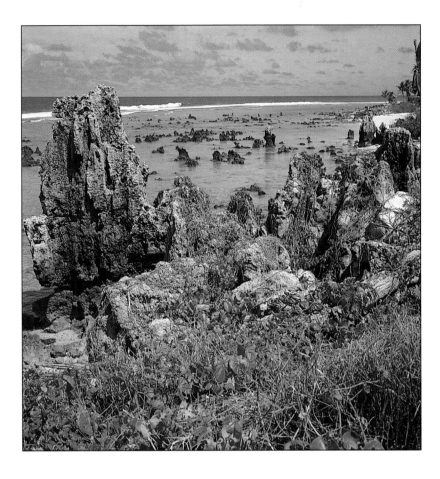

Land or sea level changes have left this coral exposed on Nauru Island in the Pacific.

Facts and figures

- *Although Australia is completely surrounded by sea, it is usually called a continent and not an island because of its huge size.*
- *The largest island in the world is Greenland. It is 840,000 square miles in area.*
- *The other nine largest islands in descending order of size are: New Guinea, Borneo, Madagascar, Baffin Island (Canada), Sumatra, Honshu (Japan), Britain, Vancouver Island (Canada), Ellesmere Island (Canada).*
- *The largest freshwater island is Marajo Island in the mouth of the Amazon River. It is about 150 miles wide by 125 miles long.*
- *The largest atoll in the world is Kwajalein in the Marshall Islands (Pacific Ocean). It is 175 miles long, enclosing a lagoon 1,100 square miles in size.*
- *The world's most remote island is Bouvet Oya in the South Atlantic. It lies more than 1,000 miles from the nearest land.*
- *The highest island mountain is Hawaii's Mauna Kea, which soars to a height of 13,700 feet.*

3. LIFE SUPPORT

The type and variety of natural life an island can support depends on the climate, the kind of soils, and what plant seeds or animals manage to reach the island to start life there.

The climate of an island varies with its latitude. The Arctic and Antarctic islands all suffer from freezing temperatures for much of the year, and this encourages little more than lichens and mosses to grow. As well as being the largest island in the world, most of Greenland lies within the Arctic Circle and so it is one of the coldest islands. Much of Greenland is covered by ice and snow all year round. Islands nearer the equator are warmer and usually are able to support more life. Borneo, in Southeast Asia, lies directly on the equator and has dense tropical forests with a huge variety of plants and animals.

Islands do have one climatic feature in common: the surrounding sea or large body of water tends to keep temperatures moderate. Water retains heat longer than land, so in colder months places near the sea tend to be warmer than those inland. The opposite is true in the warmer months—coastal areas are cooled by the sea.

The bitterly cold island of Greenland supports little natural vegetation.

Being surrounded by water can also mean a comparatively high rainfall. Britain is one example. From studies of pollen in ancient soils, it is thought that Britain's climate changed when the country became an island some 8,000 years ago. Ocean water started circulating around the land and the weather changed from a drier continental climate to a wetter one, kept moderate by the Atlantic Ocean. Evidence for this comes from the way pine, a continental tree, was replaced by the water-loving alder tree.

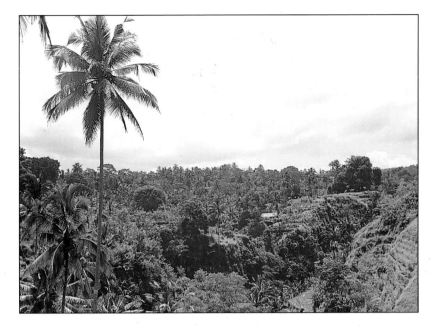

Above Lush greenery covers the warm, wet, tropical island of Bali in Indonesia.

Many islands suffer from too much rain falling at once, especially those in tropical places such as the Caribbean and Pacific areas near the equator. These regions are particularly prone to cyclones, hurricanes, and typhoons (all different kinds of tropical storms), which can be very destructive. When Hurricane Hugo struck the Caribbean island of Montserrat in 1989, it left 95 percent of the island's buildings damaged, roads washed away, and plants uprooted.

Plants need not only warmth and water to grow but also soil. A new island, such as a recently formed volcanic or coral island, starts off with bare rock. However, very quickly the wind, rain, and sun get to work in a process called

Left Hurricane damage on Caribbean islands often leaves a scene of devastation.

The bleak volcanic landscape of Ascension Island, in the Atlantic Ocean, where little plant life has been able to take root.

weathering. Gradually tiny bits of rock break up and collect in crevices. This happens all over the rocky island until there are little pockets of soil in which seeds find a foothold and grow.

Few islands remain deserts for long. Soon, from across the sea, come seeds and small animals. The wind can carry light plant seeds long distances from the mainland or a nearby island; birds bring seeds either in their droppings or perhaps stuck to their feet; floating driftwood that reaches the island may carry small animals such as ants, spiders, or beetles. Often grass and other loose plants mat together, making a seagoing platform on which larger animals sometimes travel. Reptiles tend to survive particularly well on such journeys as they have

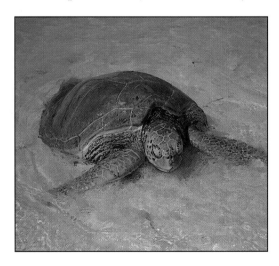

Because they can swim, turtles are often the first animals to inhabit islands.

Life after Death

A hundred years after the massive explosion of Krakatoa (see page 9), a small part of the old island still remains. Slopes that a century ago were bare volcanic rock are now covered by thick tropical forest and are full of wildlife. Seeds floated across the sea or were brought by birds. Winged animals such as birds and butterflies and other insects flew from the mainland. The rats, pythons, and lizards on the island probably arrived on logs or other floating objects.

The first plants appear on Surtsey.

watertight skin, which is not much harmed by seawater. Animals that can swim, such as turtles, are some of the first to reach and inhabit an island. If humans sail there, they can unsuspectingly bring other land animals, such as rats that have been living in the ship.

There is no knowing how fast plant life will appear and what species will take hold. Much depends on the direction of winds, how close other land lies, and what plants and animals manage to make the journey across the water. Over time, the variety and numbers will grow. On the distant but comparatively old island of Hawaii, far out in the Pacific Ocean, more than 1,700 flowering plants alone managed to reach the island by natural means. The relatively young Maldive Islands have only 87 different naturally introduced plants and about twice that number of species of animals.

The coconut
The coconut plant is very common in tropical islands because it can travel across the world by water. The coconut palm grows along the edge of tropical beaches, leaning over, so that when the coconuts fall they roll into the sea. The thick husk of the coconut allows it to float and protects the nut inside for as long as four months at sea, until it lands on a new tropical island.

Below The different ways in which plant and animal life arrives on islands.

4. FLORA AND FAUNA

Because of the different kinds of habitats on islands around the world, the plants and animals vary from thin mosses to dense tropical forests and from simple sea creatures to the thousands of more complex species that thrive in the rich vegetation of the tropics. What is different about some islands is that, because of their isolation, they have become sanctuaries for animals and plants that are found nowhere else in the world.

Sanctuaries

Some isolated islands have become sanctuaries because they have been naturally protected from changes that may have taken place elsewhere. Certain animals may still exist on a particular island because the predator (animal or human) or disease that killed them off in another place never reached the island. It might also be that there are fewer other animals competing for the same food and so there is a better chance of survival on an island.

Madagascar has a number of animals that are unique to the island. The most famous of these is the lemur, a long-tailed member of the monkey family. From fossils found on the African mainland, scientists know that lemurs once lived there too, but they died out for an unknown reason. The separation of Madagascar from the mainland has allowed the lemur to evolve without the dangers that affected it on the African continent.

Lemurs on Madagascar. They are only found there and on the nearby Comoro Islands.

The small islands off New Zealand are also home to animals that became extinct elsewhere millions of years ago. The tuatara is a very rare reptile that looks like a heavily built lizard. It is actually related to the dinosaur and not to the modern lizard. The fossilized bones of an identical creature have been found in two-million-year-old rocks.

Another island that acts like a sanctuary is Aldabra in the Seychelles. One animal that lives there is the booby, a bird like a gannet. These birds fly for hundreds of miles searching for schools of fish; they spend most of the year in the air. However, their chosen nesting site is Aldabra, one of the few uninhabited islands in the area that is virtually free of cats, rats, and other creatures that might eat their eggs or chicks.

Evolution

The isolation of islands not only protects plants and animals from dying out but can also create a special environment where flora and fauna can evolve in a way different from that anywhere else in the world. Because evolutionary changes on an island are not affected by large numbers of species as they are on the mainland, the speed of evolution is usually faster on islands than elsewhere. Islands become small inbred communities of plants and animals.

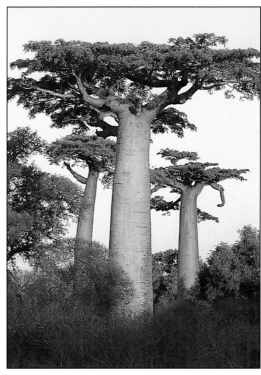

Above Nine types of these strange baobab trees grow on Madagascar. On the African mainland, only one type grows.

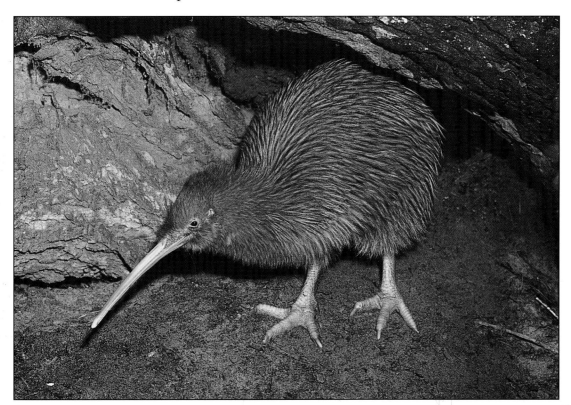

Left Flightless birds, like this kiwi in New Zealand, evolved on many islands that were free from predators.

When not basking on rocks, the iguanas of the Galapagos Islands spend much of their time in the sea.

The Galapagos Islands off the west coast of South America are home to several creatures that have evolved in a unique way. In particular are the 13 species of finch found on the Galapagos and nowhere else. It is thought that thousands of years ago a few were blown there from the mainland by a freak storm. The islands have varied habitats, from desert areas to thick bush and high volcanic peaks, and the finches evolved and adapted to the different environments they found. Some finches have heavy beaks for crushing fruit, others have slim beaks to pick off insects, and one species even uses its beak to cut a cactus spine and push it into holes to get beetle grubs.

Other animals found on the Galapagos are marine iguanas, huge tortoises, and flightless cormorants. Marine iguanas are the only lizards in the world that regularly spend time in the sea (they eat seaweed). Flightless birds are common on many remote oceanic islands. Aldabra, for example, is home to the small rail bird, which has similar cousins on mainland Africa. But the difference is that on Aldabra the rail cannot fly. On the mainland rails have many enemies and need wings to escape, but on Aldabra, where there are no animal predators, the bird has evolved without wings.

Probably the most famous of all flightless birds is the now extinct dodo, which used to live on the island of Mauritius in the Indian Ocean. It was a pigeon-like bird that grew to the size of a turkey and shed its wings as it evolved in isolation. New Zealand has its own version that has survived, the kiwi, which is the country's national symbol.

Giant tortoises are other animals that have commonly evolved on remote islands. Madagascar and Aldabra are two of the places where they are found. The giant ones are probably descended from normal-sized tortoises that may have arrived on driftwood from the mainland. Tortoises have been found floating at sea, so it seems they can survive the long sea journey. It is not known exactly why they grow so large, but it is possible that since there are no predators they just live longer and get bigger.

Growing to a large size is not restricted to tortoises. A hundred years ago, there were tales of a monster on the islands of Indonesia that attacked humans. Known as the Komodo dragon, the creature is in fact an overgrown monitor (a kind of lizard common in tropical countries). It grows up to 10 feet in length, is much bulkier than a normal monitor, and eats meat. Because there are no other large meat-eating creatures to prey on pigs and deer on the island of Komodo, the lizard may have taken advantage of this abundant source of food and evolved into a larger animal.

A giant Galapagos tortoise

Galapagos

The Galapagos Islands lie on the equator, 600 miles west of the coast of South America. The islands are the peaks of gigantic volcanoes, rising 6,500 to 10,000 feet from the seabed. There are six main islands, two of which are uninhabited, and over fifty smaller islands and islets. Many of the creatures on the islands are unique because they evolved in different ways from their ancestors on the South American continent. A quarter of the shore fish, half the plants, and almost all the reptiles are only found here. Since no large land mammals reached the islands, reptiles have become the dominant creatures, just as they were all over the world in the very distant past.

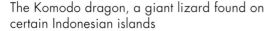

The Komodo dragon, a giant lizard found on certain Indonesian islands

5. ISLAND PEOPLES

Like the plants and animals that inhabit islands, some island people have also developed their own particular characteristics. Being isolated and having little contact with others, they sometimes have languages, beliefs, and traditions that are not found elsewhere. But over the last few hundred years, most islands have been visited by outsiders and, with modern transportation and communications, few are still cut off from the world. This has meant changes for islanders as they adapt and learn about people elsewhere. Few are able to keep their traditional way of life as it once was.

Iceland is an island with one of the most homogeneous peoples in the world. It is a cold and isolated island in the North Atlantic that was settled by descendants of Nordic explorers and traders, the Vikings. There has been virtually no immigration to the island since it was first settled. In their isolation the Icelandic people developed their own culture, rich with sagas and poetry, and their language, related to Old English, is much as it was spoken originally.

On the other side of the world, in the warmth of the Pacific Ocean, live the Polynesians. Polynesians have light skins compared with other Pacific islanders such as Melanesians. Polynesians are tall and well

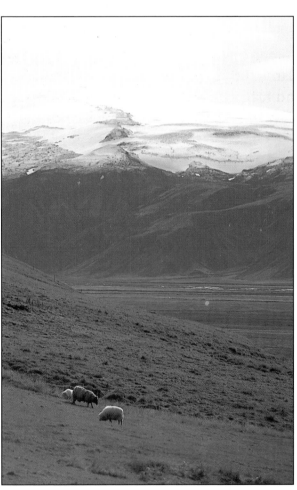

Above Iceland, home to descendants of Viking explorers

Left Polynesian girls from the Cook Islands in the South Pacific

20

built, mostly with straight dark hair, and they all speak dialects of one language. This suggests that the Polynesians all came from one direction over a short period of time and had little chance to mix with other races. It remains a puzzle whether they originally came island-hopping eastward from Asia or westward across the vast ocean from the Americas.

Polynesians were and still are hardy seafarers, and they were culturally and technically advanced when they made their first journeys around the Pacific Islands. Where there was wood, they built strong houses and boats that they carved and decorated. They used wood and stone for tools, skins and the plant fibers to make clothes, and farmed the land, using fruits and other plants they took from island to island. As well as hunting and fishing, Polynesians domesticated animals like dogs, pigs, and chickens. On many islands, they built stone altars where they worshiped their ancestors. On some remote islands, their traditional ways of life still remain largely untouched.

Also in the Pacific region lies the island of New Guinea. There are mountain tribes in the interior that have only recently come into contact with the outside

A dancer performing one of Bali's traditional dances. The Indonesian island still preserves its rich culture.

Easter Island
Some 2,500 miles from South America and 1,500 miles from the nearest inhabited island lies mysterious Easter Island. Scattered around the island are tall stone statues. Polynesian islanders used to light fires and worship in front of these statues. Nobody knows how the islanders managed to transport and erect the enormous slabs of stone.

The stone statues of Easter Island

world. Probably related to the earliest settlers from Asia about 40,000 years ago, these people are very short with dark skins, tightly curled hair, and features common to many African peoples. Their Stone Age existence as hunter-gatherers has been preserved because of the remoteness of their valley homes, hidden in the dense tropical forests of this island.

Mixed races

When European explorers reached the Pacific Islands in the 1700s, they brought trade and slave labor. Many people of the Pacific area were moved from island to island, and the different races mixed. This is true in the history of many parts of the world as international trade grew, and islands were settled by outsiders.

In the Indian Ocean, the Seychelles Islands were used as bases by pirates until the French claimed the islands in 1754. Africans were captured and brought to work on the plantations as slaves. Later the British took control, and when slavery was abolished in 1833, they brought in Indian and Chinese laborers to do the work. Today the people of the Seychelles have every shade of skin and hair imaginable, because they are a mixture of African, Indian, Chinese, Arab, and European blood.

Madagascar's native people, probably of Asian origin, first came into contact with outsiders about A.D. 900 when Arab traders arrived. The traders settled and brought in African slaves. Later, Europeans took control of the island,

Mutiny on the *Bounty*
One strange island story concerns the sailors on a British Royal Naval ship, the HMS Bounty. *After setting their captain adrift in a longboat, the remaining crew sailed away and no one knew what became of them. Many years later, on Pitcairn Island in the South Pacific, a race of half English and half native people was found—the descendants of the* **Bounty** *mutineers.*

The people of Lake Titicaca in Peru have built homes on floating islands of reeds in the middle of the lake.

The voyage of Kon Tiki
Scientists do not agree on where the Polynesians came from. The traditional view is that the Polynesians spread from Asia east across the Pacific. But Thor Heyerdahl, a Norwegian ethnologist, believed they came westward from the Americas. To prove his theory, he set out from Peru, in South America, on a balsa-wood raft called **Kon Tiki**. *He reached Polynesia and proved that the winds and currents in the Pacific made it more likely that the Polynesians came from the Americas. It is also true that the native people of Polynesia and the Americas have similar physical appearances, similar styles of religious worship, and certain language similarities.*

but they did not become the dominant race in Madagascar as they did on some other islands such as New Zealand.

The islands of the Caribbean have seen dramatic changes in their people. Thought to have come to the islands about 1,500 years ago, the Arawaks were relatively peaceful farmers and fishermen. However, an aggressive tribe, the Caribs, arrived and ferociously attacked the Arawaks. The Caribs were fighters and fine canoeists; they killed the Arawaks and took the females as slaves. Their advance across the islands was halted in the late 1400s by the arrival of Europeans, who virtually wiped out both Arawaks and Caribs. The Europeans settled and brought in thousands of Africans to work on plantations as slaves. Later they imported laborers from Asia. Although the islands have mixed races, Africans are dominant in the region both in numbers and culturally.

Carnival on the island of Trinidad, in the Caribbean

23

6. ISLAND EXPLORERS AND SCIENTISTS

Polynesians

Islanders themselves usually are good explorers because, being surrounded by water, they are often experienced sailors. The original Polynesian islanders were such a people. It is thought that the Society Islands (these include Tahiti) were their base, and from there they spread out north to Hawaii and south to New Zealand, where they became known as the Maoris. Their greatest travels were probably from about A.D. 800 onward. There are no records of their voyages, just the evidence of how far the Polynesian race spread.

Although they were good boat builders and navigators, the Polynesians must have been immensely brave to set out into unknown seas without a compass or map. The Pacific Ocean is vast, and they would have sailed for weeks and sometimes months not knowing where they were heading and without seeing land. Their dugout canoes could be up to one hundred feet long and usually had stabilizers called outriggers. The Polynesians were looking for new lands to colonize, and on board were men, women, children, animals, and plants, as well as food and water for the journey.

Polynesians use outriggers to stabilize their boats, in much the same way as their seafaring ancestors.

Christopher Columbus lands on a Caribbean island, believing it to be in the East Indies.

European explorers and traders

People set out from all over the world to explore distant islands. The Arabs and Chinese visited many of the islands of the Indian Ocean and Southeast Asia, but it was European explorers, setting forth on great sea journeys in the early fifteenth century, who began to keep careful records and to chart even the most remote of the world's islands.

The first wave of European explorers set out in the hope of finding riches and trade. They wanted to find sea routes to the famed Spice Islands of the East Indies. In Europe there was a huge demand for spices (such as cloves and cinnamon) and silk cloth, and most of the trade was controlled by Arab merchants who sailed the Indian Ocean. With new, improved methods of shipbuilding, Europeans thought they could reach the East Indies themselves and buy direct from the islanders.

Traveling west across the Atlantic, Christopher Columbus searched for a route to the East Indies and China. He arrived in the Caribbean islands in 1492. He thought he had reached the East Indies, but in fact the first Europeans to get to the East Indies were the Portuguese, who sailed around the African continent and across the Indian Ocean. The Portuguese found islands such as the Moluccas, Sumatra, Java, and Sri Lanka, and

Spices
Spices originally only grew in southern and southeastern Asia. Cinnamon was grown on the island of Sri Lanka; the Moluccas were renowned for their nutmeg and cloves; and pepper grew on most of the islands. In Europe, these spices were used to preserve meat through the winter and to flavor foods. They were also being used for medicines. Spices were extremely valuable to Europeans, and the search for spices and trade with island producers was as valuable as the quest for gold.

they began trading in precious stones, pepper, cinnamon, cloves, and sandalwood. All the European nations wanted a share of this rich East Indies trade, but the Dutch became the most successful. Within a hundred years they had taken over from the Portuguese as the main traders.

This was not a happy time for the islanders themselves, for there were constant attacks on local rulers as well as fighting among the Europeans. Just to prevent other countries from buying cloves, the Dutch laid waste to the Banda Islands, a major source of spice, killing 15,000 people and enslaving the rest. Then, in 1625, they destroyed all the clove trees on the Moluccas except for the one island in their possession.

European scientific explorers

The last major island group to be explored by Europeans were the Pacific islands, the most numerous and the most distant. Captain James Cook, an Englishman, led a series of long expeditions across the Pacific Ocean from 1768 onward. This was the beginning of a new stage in European exploration with part of the reason for the expeditions being scientific curiosity.

On board Cook's ships were biologists and naturalists who wanted to explore the remote islands in order to learn about their flora and fauna. One of the biologists on board was Joseph Banks, who brought back a large collection of butterflies, insects, and plants. Captain Cook was also testing navigational equipment that proved vital for charting the exact position of some of these islands.

Captain Cook's ships arrive at Tahiti, in the Pacific Ocean, in 1773.

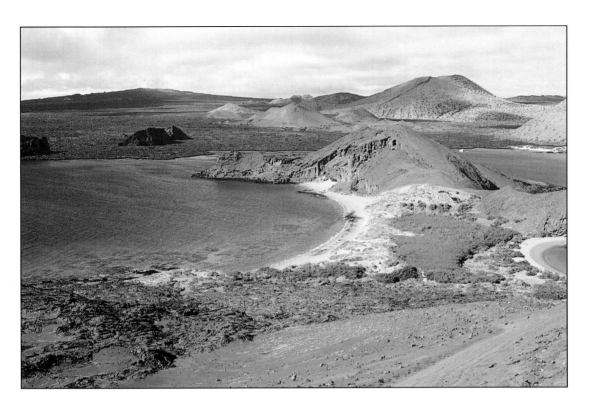

Islands as unique habitats were first properly explored by two naturalists, Charles Darwin and Alfred Wallace. In 1832 Darwin set off on the HMS *Beagle* around the world and made a number of visits to the Galapagos Islands. He noticed that the animals of the islands resembled those of South America, but many had strange features. He wondered why they were not the same as the continental animals and gradually formed his theory of evolution, which he published in a book, *On the Origin of the Species,* in 1859. At the same time, Wallace, in Indonesia, had come to the same conclusions from his studies of wildlife on the islands in that part of the world. Although their theories are widely accepted today, in the mid-nineteenth century they were regarded as revolutionary.

Today, islands are still being explored, mostly by scientists. Because remote islands are isolated, the plant and animal life is little influenced by outside forces. This makes island systems of wildlife easier to study than those of a whole continent. As a result, islands like Aldabra have become particularly important places for the study of the relationships between plants and animals and their habitats.

7. HUMAN INTERFERENCE

In many cases, exploration by humans brought about much more dramatic changes in the wildlife of islands than was caused by natural evolution. And the changes occurred in a much shorter space of time.

The great Polynesian explorers were to have lasting effects in New Zealand. When the Maoris arrived there, they found a fertile land containing large animals and the flightless birds called moas. The Maoris hunted the moas for their meat and used their skins for clothing, cleared their natural forest habitat, and brought rats and dogs that ate the birds' chicks and eggs. The arrival of Europeans in New Zealand, 200 years ago, added to this disruption, with the cutting down of forests and introduction of sheep to graze the land. Within a few centuries of human arrival, all the moas in New Zealand were extinct except the kiwi, which is the last remaining species.

New Zealand's flora and fauna have been changed since land was cleared and non-native animals like sheep were introduced.

Huge areas of forest in Sumatra have been cut down to make way for crops.

A similar fate befell the giant tortoises of the islands of the Indian Ocean, except on Aldabra, which lay far off the main trade routes. In the early days of exploration, there was no way fresh meat could be kept on long sea journeys. The tortoises of the islands not only provided a meal for sailors who visited the islands but some tortoises could also be kept alive aboard ship so that fresh meat was available. Eventually whole tortoise populations were wiped out on these islands.

Human suffering
It is not just animals that are affected when new people arrive on an island. On many islands in the Caribbean, where Europeans landed and settled, the whole Arawak population was wiped out within 50 years. The Arawaks were killed by a combination of disease and hardships imposed by the Europeans. Today, in Kalimantan on the island of Borneo, there is massive deforestation, with the result that the native forest home of the Punan tribespeople is being destroyed, and they are having difficulty surviving.

Almost every island on earth has some species that humans have
introduced. Some were brought deliberately, either to breed for food or
to control pests that newcomers found on islands. Other species arrived
by accident.

The most common animals introduced to islands were those that settlers
were used to breeding at home, such as pigs, goats, chickens, and rabbits.
They also brought dogs and cats, and, unknowingly, rats that were living in
the holds of ships. Some of these animals remained domesticated, but others
became wild and caused great ecological changes such as on the Ascension
Islands, where wild goats have stripped areas bare of vegetation.

There is probably no more altered island habitat than New Zealand. Of
some 53 attempts to introduce new mammals, 34 became established in the
wild, and these gradually took the place of many of New Zealand's native
species. It seems that despite being well-adapted to their island, native animals
do not survive the arrival of newcomers to their habitat and to the
competition that they bring.

There were no native freshwater fish in New Zealand's rivers, so they were
stocked with trout from Britain. The nonindigenous rabbit became a pest

when it bred in the wild and started eating crops, so weasels were introduced and let loose to control the rabbits. Deer have thrived so well that they are causing terrible damage to vegetation and are now classed as vermin. However, humans did bring some useful creatures, such as honey bees.

Introducing an animal to control another is not always a success. In the Caribbean, the mongoose was brought in to control the rat population on the islands. It did that very well, but mongooses then bred and started eating native reptiles and birds. Some native species have become extinct as a result. On Moorea, in the Pacific, there once lived the small partula snail. The giant African snail was introduced to the island, but it began eating the crops. So another species of meat-eating snail was brought in to eat the giant snails. Unfortunately it ate the partula, too.

The dodo

The dodo was a flightless bird that lived on Mauritius. Portuguese explorers who landed there called it **duodo***, which means simpleton in Portuguese. They called it this because it trusted people so much it would run to them and could be knocked on the head and killed. For sailors it was a valuable source of food on long sea journeys. They killed the last dodo in 1681. The bird is now extinct.*

8. AN ISLAND LIVING

About 10 percent of the world's population live on islands. Some like Japan, Britain, Java, and Hong Kong are densely populated. Some island nations have become extremely powerful and successful. As well as the larger wealthy nations like Japan and Britain, there are also tiny, very rich islands like Hong Kong and Singapore. The last two both lie just off the coast of mainland Asia and have become leading world financial and trading centers. It is partly their location on important communication routes around the world that has helped them to succeed. Islands such as Sri Lanka and Hawaii have also benefited from lying at strategic points on air and sea routes.

One of the advantages islanders have for making a living is a good supply of fish in the sea around them. As well as providing food, surplus fish can be sold and traded for other goods that may be in short supply on an island

Above Singapore is a Chinese-run modern island city in Southeast Asia.

Left Icelandic fishing boats. Many islanders depend on fishing for part of their livelihood.

The people of South Uist, in the Outer Hebrides, survive by stock raising, small family farming, and fishing.

with limited resources. The settlement of the bleak Canadian island of Newfoundland was entirely based on the rich catches of codfish in the seas offshore. It was the same for settlers on remote islands such as the Falkland Islands and South Georgia in the South Atlantic. The large population on the islands of the Pacific could not survive without fishing, and in the Indian Ocean, for example, the Seychelles islanders catch tuna, can it, and export it.

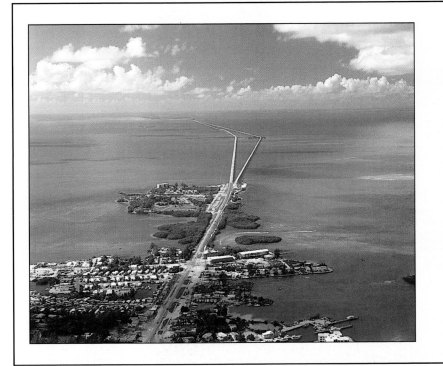

The Florida Keys, islands off the southern tip of Florida, are linked by road bridges across the sea.

Water shortages

Like many small islands around the world, Key West in Florida, an island that is home to the most southerly city in the United States, suffers from a lack of fresh water. Desalination plants have been built to convert seawater to drinking water. Other poorer island communities around the world cannot afford this expensive way of ensuring there is enough water.

Plantation crops

The more remote the island, the more people are likely to exist at a subsistence level, growing food crops, perhaps raising a few animals, and fishing. But on many of the islands that were colonized by Europeans, plantation crops such as sugar, coffee, and bananas were introduced. These cash crops were and still are sold for export worldwide. In the early days, the majority of islanders would not have have reaped the benefits of the plantation crops; the profits would have gone to the rich European plantation owners, some of whom may not have even lived on the island.

The economies of many islands were often dominated by plantation crops. The problem was then that if demand fell or, as sometimes happened, a cyclone destroyed the harvest, the islanders would have no other way to make

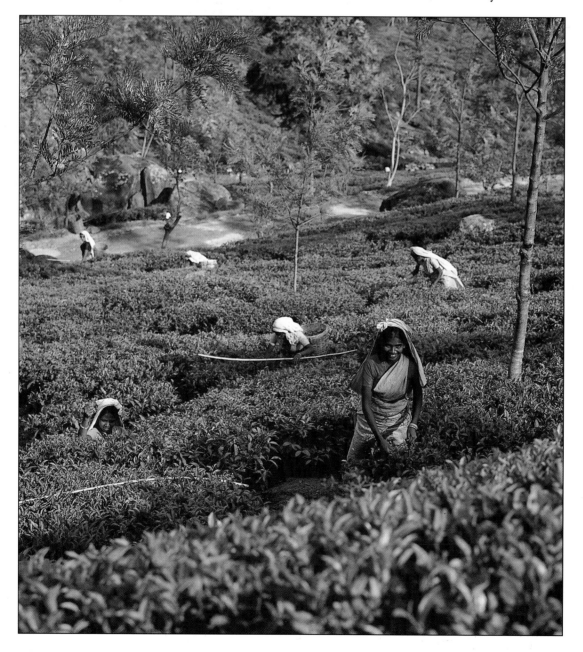

Picking tea on a plantation in Sri Lanka.

a living. Cuba, in the Caribbean, and Mauritius, in the Indian Ocean, were two such islands that depended on growing sugarcane. Now the islanders have tried to introduce other crops and industries to help balance their economies.

The island of Sri Lanka off the south coast of India grows tea, rubber, and coconuts. It has to import some of its basic foodstuff, rice, and still depends on the unreliable world market to make money out of its cash crops. In Papua New Guinea, little space has been left for the crops people need to grow to eat because so many cash crops such as coffee, cocoa, and coconut are being grown.

Some islands have rich natural resources. But seldom have the islanders themselves been allowed to control and use these resources; more often they have been exploited by larger and wealthier countries. Borneo is thickly covered in tropical forest, but the island is being stripped of its wood, mainly by the Indonesian government, to sell to meet the Japanese demand for hardwoods. In Papua New Guinea there is a huge copper mine, but it is not owned by the local people. They have had little more than jobs as poorly paid workers in the mine.

Yachts in the harbor at Antigua, in the Caribbean, where tourism is a major source of income.

Tourism

One of the most important sources of income for islands today is tourism. It is not only the beautiful islands with sandy beaches and palm trees that attract tourists. There is also a growing interest in visiting islands with curious natural features such as the wildlife of the Galapagos and the splendid volcanic scenery of Iceland. Cheaper air travel is one of the main factors that has made it possible for people to reach some of the world's remote and interesting islands.

Some of the main island groups that rely on tourism are the Caribbean islands, the islands of the Seychelles and Maldives in the Indian Ocean, the Pacific islands, the Canary Islands in the Atlantic, and the many islands of the Mediterranean Sea.

Tourism has brought jobs (such as in hotels, banks, stores, and restaurants) and money to many of these islands, so that local standards of living have risen. In the Seychelles, local people have given up farming and fishing and about 20 percent of the workforce is now employed in better paid jobs in tourism.

However, tourism does have its drawbacks. Some islands have become so dependent on tourism for their economy that if tourists are put off from coming to the island for any reason (perhaps political trouble or a natural disaster like a hurricane), the economy slumps. If this happens, islanders seldom desire or are able to return to farming and fishing.

It is not always the local people who benefit from tourism. The greater part of the price of a package vacation goes to the foreign operator; in some cases, hotels are owned by a foreign travel company, and so the profits go back to the company's country of origin. Although tourism means that new buildings, roads, and airports have to be built, which helps local businesses, it also means land is lost for agricultural use. In addition, many new building developments are very ugly. On the other hand, historic buildings that might otherwise fall into disrepair may be preserved for tourists to visit.

Tourism also brings a change in lifestyle and traditions for islanders. The island of Bali, in Indonesia, has a particularly rich cultural history, which is one reason why tourists visit the island. The islanders put on special performances of their dances for tourists and sell handicrafts. Some say tourism has helped preserve the customs, ceremonies, and arts of the island; others say the Balinese culture is dead because it is now just a moneymaking business.

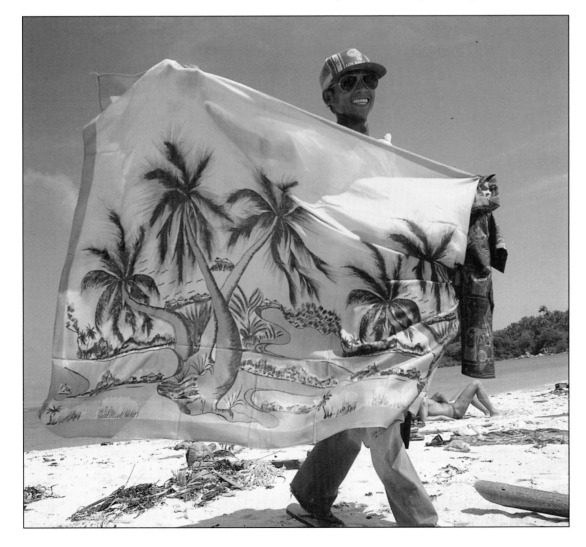

Local boys make money selling towels to tourists on the island of Samui, Thailand.

9. CONTROL AND OWNERSHIP

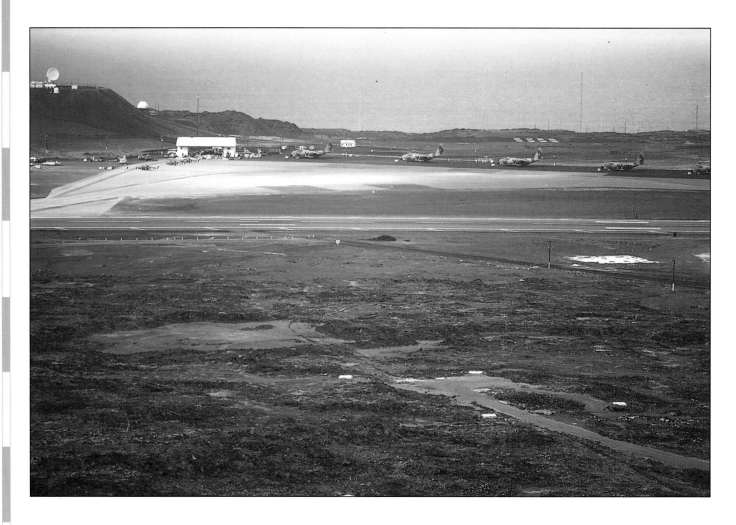

In addition to Australia which, because of its vast size, is usually considered to be a continent and not an island, there are nine large nations in the world that consist entirely of islands. These are Indonesia, Japan, Philippines, New Zealand, Sri Lanka, Madagascar, Great Britain, Iceland, and Cuba. The largest in population and in area is Indonesia: in total it is almost the size of Greenland, but it is made up of 13,677 islands. Some 6,000 of these are inhabited, and the population is the fifth biggest in the world. Greenland, the world's largest island, belongs to Denmark, though it is largely self-governing and may soon achieve independence. There are also hundreds of small islands, especially in the Caribbean and the Pacific, that are countries in their own right.

An air force base on Ascension Island. The island serves as an important communications base in the middle of the Atlantic Ocean.

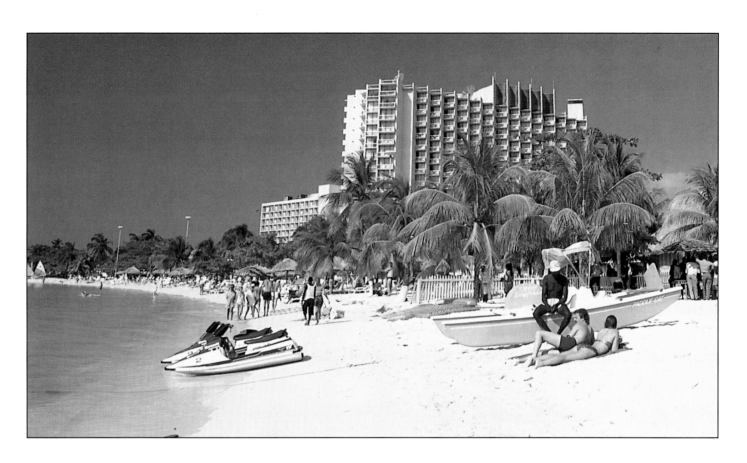

Throughout history wars have been fought for islands. Who now inhabits and controls an island depends very much on that island's history. Almost all islands were at one time colonies of European countries, although many have now achieved their independence and are self-governing.

Above Jamaica was first occupied by Arawaks and then the Spanish. It later fell to the British, who imported Africans to work the plantations. The island became independent from Britain in 1962.

Left A Greek sign reminds people of the struggle with Turkey for control of the island of Cyprus, in the eastern Mediterranean.

The Falkland Islands still belong to Great Britain, even though they lie thousands of miles away in the South Atlantic.

The Caribbean was one area in particular where islands frequently changed hands. After Columbus landed in 1492, Spanish settlers arrived and started colonies on the islands. They were followed by British, French, Dutch, Danes, and other Europeans, who grabbed islands as their footholds in the New World. Wars in Europe over the following centuries, and rivalry in the Caribbean, meant continual battles for control of the islands. Things settled down in the 1800s, and during the 1900s many islands gained independence from their colonial rulers. There are now 24 separate states in the Caribbean.

Some islands, such as Hispaniola in the Caribbean, have a split ownership. The eastern part of Hispaniola is the French-speaking Republic of Haiti, and the western half is the Spanish-speaking Dominican Republic, which has close links with the United States. New Guinea, in Southeast Asia, is divided between Irian Jaya, belonging to Indonesia, and the independent state of Papua New Guinea. In the same area is Borneo, an island divided in three: the independent state of Brunei; the states of Sabah and Sarawak, which belong to

Malaysia; and Kalimantan, which is owned by Indonesia. In the Mediterranean is the tiny island of Cyprus. It has been partitioned since 1974 between Turkey and Greece, because each nation claims to be the rightful owner.

Often islands are occupied not only for the resources such as minerals or wood that they can provide but also because they add to a country's territory. Or they may be in a strategic position or a useful communications base. For example Hong Kong and the Falkland Islands have always been useful bases in far-flung parts of the world for Great Britain, as have Guam (in the north Pacific) and Hawaii (prior to its becoming a state in 1959) for the United States. France keeps hold of the islands in Tahiti-Polynesia and uses outlying ones for nuclear tests.

Supposedly independent islands often rely on powerful foreign countries for help or aid. The Philippines have for a long time been supported financially by the United States and in return the U.S. government, until recently, sited huge military bases there. Payments are made to the Seychelles government for the use of land for a United States satellite tracking station, and Cuba was sustained for many years by the former Soviet Union, which helped the island economically and kept military forces on the island.

After 155 years of British ownership, the busy island of Hong Kong will be returned to China in 1997.

10. ENVIRONMENT AND SURVIVAL

Like all habitats, islands are under environmental threat from misuse or overuse by humans. The small size of most islands means that harm can occur quickly and have devastating effects if the situation is not controlled.

On less developed islands, tourism can bring additional pressures where there is already a shortage of resources such as gas, coal, or electric power. Water is a particular problem for many islands that are popular with tourists. One solution is to build desalination plants to use the water from the sea, but these are very expensive for developing countries. Tourism can also bring pollution because the sewage systems are unable to cope with the additional number of people, and uncleared garbage left by tourists often accumulates on beaches.

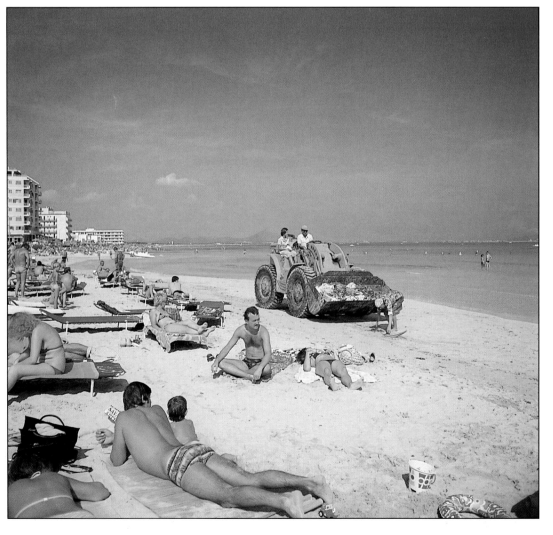

Trash has to be cleared regularly from the crowded tourist beaches on the Mediterranean island of Majorca.

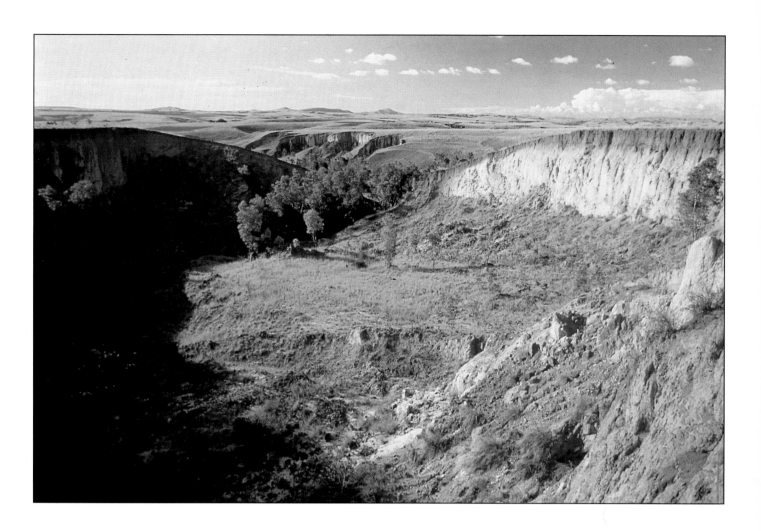

Soil erosion is particularly bad on Madagascar, where trees have been cleared for farming.

Tourism can have good and bad effects on the flora and fauna of islands. Sometimes tourism encourages the preservation of rare animals, such as the lemurs of Madagascar, in wildlife sanctuaries for visitors to see. In the Florida Keys, islands lying off the coast of Florida near Miami, there are many state and country parks where coral and other marine animals are protected. On the other hand, tourism results in harm when coral or large sea shells are bought as souvenirs, and around many islands the sea has been stripped of large shellfish to meet the demand. Coral is in danger all over the world because it is particularly sensitive to changes in its environment, and the slightest pollution in the water is enough to stop its growth.

Plantation agriculture has caused environmental damage because it requires that almost all the natural vegetation be removed before planting begins. Mauritius has virtually no natural woodland left. Hawaii is suffering from soil erosion due to clearing the land of its natural cover and plowing for pineapple planting. Overgrazing by livestock has caused soil erosion on islands such as Madagascar, where vast areas of forest were cleared in order to make pasture for cattle introduced from Africa.

Other islands where there has been serious deforestation are Sumatra and Borneo. It is thought that overall in Indonesia, more than one third of all the

Atomic testing

France has carried out more than 80 nuclear tests on the island of Moruroa in the South Pacific. It was hoped that the island was so remote that the tests would do no harm. Because of testing nuclear weapons by exploding them underground, the island has begun to sink and is now five feet lower than it used to be. The whole island has been weakened, and radioactivity is leaking into the sea through a crack in the atoll. Tropical storms make matters worse. The radioactivity concentrates in seafood, the main diet of Pacific people, and can produce cancer and other serious illnesses.

An underwater explosion during atomic tests in Bikini lagoon, in the Pacific Ocean

tropical forest has been chopped down since 1950. The effects can be devastating for the environment: wildlife dies when it loses its natural habitat, soil erodes without vegetation cover, flooding occurs, and there may even be local climate changes. Problems like these are often recognized on underdeveloped islands but they are not being tackled, partly through a short-term desire to make money.

The seas around islands are under pressure too. Overfishing is a worldwide problem that not only harms the natural balance of life in the sea but also affects the livelihood and survival of island people. Nowadays fishing island-nations like Iceland, Great Britain, and Japan have huge factory trawlers that catch millions of tons of fish a year. In the North Atlantic, stocks of fish have fallen dramatically in the last few years, and there are now controls on the amount of fish that are allowed to be caught.

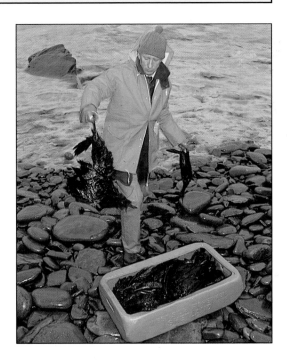

Oil-covered birds were casualties after a tanker went aground off the Shetland Islands, in the North Atlantic, in 1993.

The size of modern ships and their potentially dangerous cargoes are a worry for islanders. In the Shetland Islands, off the coast of Scotland, there was a near disaster when an oil tanker went aground in rough seas in 1993. With their hidden coral reefs, the Pacific Islands have seen thousands of shipwrecks over the years. For many years at Key West in Florida, the most important industry was salvaging cargo from ships that had foundered on nearby reefs.

In some ways, developed, industrialized islands such as Great Britain and Japan face the most severe environmental problems. The problems are the sort that are found in any overcrowded part of our planet—in particular, air, water, and soil pollution from industry and agriculture. The difference is that the effects of these problems are magnified because Great Britain and Japan are islands, and the environment has tight limits on how much it can take.

However, such rich nations can afford to take the costly measures needed to control environmental problems. These nations are also spending time and money looking at solutions in order that humans can live safely in increasingly crowded and limited places such as islands. Studying islands and the relationships between the animals, plants, and environment may show us a way forward for our whole planet, which is, after all, one huge island in space.

A peaceful island far from land: Moorea, in the South Pacific, is a favorite haven for tourists.

GLOSSARY

Atoll   A circle of coral reefs.

Cash crops   Crops grown for sale, rather than for living on.

Colony   Land settled and controlled by a powerful country.

Continent   A very large landmass.

Deforestation   The cutting down and clearing of trees from land.

Delta   A flat, fan-shaped area of land near the mouth of a river, where the main stream splits into many channels at the end of its course.

Desalination   The process of removing salt, especially from seawater.

Dialects   Local accents.

Ecologies   The ways in which living things relate to each other and their environment.

Erosion   The process of being washed or blown away.

Ethnologist   Someone who studies the behavior of animals.

Evolve   To gradually change over a long period of time. As plants and animals evolve, new characteristics develop, and eventually new species arise. This gradual change is called evolution.

Extinct   No longer living. When a species of living thing dies out completely, it is extinct.

Fauna   All the animal life of a particular place or time.

Flora   All the plant life of a particular place or time.

Fossils   The remains, traces, or impressions of animals found preserved in rock.

Immigration   Moving from one country to live permanently in another.

Inbred   Bred from closely related parents.

Islets   Very small islands.

Lagoon   A stretch of water cut off from the open sea by coral reefs or sandbars.

Latitude   The distance of a place north or south of the equator.

Lava   Molten rock from inside the earth that pours out of a volcano.

Lichen   Plant made up of an alge and a fungus. It typically grows on the surface of rocks and tree trunks.

New World   An old term for North and South America.

Plantations   Estates, especially in tropical countries, where cash crops such as rubber, tea, and cotton are grown on a large scale for sale.

Pollution   Poisonous substances released into air, water, and land that may upset the natural balance of the environment.

Predator   A creature that hunts and kills another.

Radioactivity   The giving out of energy in the form of dangerous rays.

Reef   A ridge of rocks, sand, or coral, the top of which lies close to the surface of the sea.

Sagas   Ancient stories, often about battles, warrior gods, and heroes.

Sanctuaries   Places of refuge or safety.

Sediment   Fine particles of mud and earth that are deposited by water.

Sewage   Waste material and liquid from factories and houses, carried in drains and sewers.

Soviet Union   A former group of republics in Eastern Europe and northern Asia controlled from Moscow. The Soviet Union broke up into separate states in 1991.

Species   A group of plants or animals with similar characteristics that can reproduce more of their kind.

Stone Age   The earliest period in human history.

Strait   A narrow channel of sea linking two larger areas of sea.

Strategic   To be in a well-placed position.

Stratosphere   An upper region or layer of the atmosphere, high above the earth's surface.

Subsistence level   A level of income that will only buy the basic needs of life, such as food.

Vermin   Troublesome or destructive animals such as mice or rats.

FURTHER READING

Bender, Lionel. *Island.* The Story of the Earth. New York: Franklin Watts, 1989.

Schafer, Susan. *The Galapagos Tortoise.* Remarkable Animals. New York: Dillon Press, 1992.

Dixon, Dougal. *The Changing Earth.* Young Geographer. New York: Thomson Learning, 1993.

Hooper, Rosanne. *Life in the Islands.* New York: Scholastic, 1994.

Lampton, Christopher. *Coral Reefs in Danger.* Brookfield, CT: Millbrook Press, 1992.

Millea, Nicholas. *Settlements.* Young Geographer. New York: Thomson Learning, 1993.

Steele, Philip. *Thor Heyerdahl and the Kon-Tiki Voyage.* Great 20th-Century Expeditions. New York: Dillon Press, 1993.

Wright, Sarah B. *Islands of the Northeastern United States and Eastern Canada.* Atlanta: Peachtree Publishers, 1990.

Other sources of information are travel and geography books about specific groups of islands, for example, the Hawaiian Islands, the Caribbean islands, Greek islands, Pacific islands, Canary Islands, Indonesia, Philippines, and Seychelles. It is also worth looking at books about volcanoes and coral for background information.

FURTHER INFORMATION

For further information about animals and their habitats that are under threat, contact the following environmental organizations:

Center for Environmental Education, Center for Marine Conservation, 1725 De Sales Street NW, Suite 500, Washington, DC 20036

Friends of the Earth (U.S.A.), 218 D Street SE, Washington, D.C. 20003

Greenpeace U.S.A., 1436 U Street NW, Washington, DC 20009

World Wildlife Fund, 1250 24th Street NW, Washington DC 20037

These organizations all campaign to protect wildlife and habitats throughout the world.

Picture acknowledgments

Britstock-IFA *cover,* Eye Ubiquitous/J. Davis 5(top), 5(lower), /J. Davis 8, 12, 20(top), /D. Brannigan 21(top), /E. Enstone 23(lower), /J. Davis 24, 29, /D. Cumming 32(top), /B. Adams 36, /J. Hulme 37, /J. Davis 39; Frank Lane Picture Library 9, /W.Wisniewski 18, 27(lower), /S. Jonasson 32(lower); NHPA /P. Johnson 14(top), 17(lower), /K. Switak 19(top), /H. Palo 27(top), /D. Woodfall 33(top), /P. Johnson 38; Still Pictures /D. Harms 7, /Y. Lefevre 15, /T. Thomas 16, /Deulefeu 17(top), /R. Seitre 19(lower), /Michel Gunther 43, /Mark Edwards 44(lower); Topham Picture Library 11, 13(top), 14(lower, both), 20 lower), 21(lower), 22, 23(top), 25, 30, 31, 34, 35, 42, 44(top); Julia Waterlow 39(lower), 41; Wayland Picture Library title page, 13(lower), 26, 28, /D. Cumming 39(top); Zefa 10, 33(lower), 40, 45. Maps and diagrams on pages 4, 6, 10 Peter Bull, and 15 John Yates.

INDEX

Numbers in **bold** refer to photographs